INTRODUCTION

Children with special educational needs (SEN) experience learning disabilities and disorders. Dyslexia, dyscalculia, and dyspraxia are some of the most common learning disorders in children. In addition, children with medical disorders such as attention deficit hyperactivity disorder (ADHD) and autism will also experience learning disruptions.

Learning disorders and disabilities are caused by disease-related abnormalities, injuries, and impairments. When it comes to schoolwork and personal organization, children with SEN will face challenges. They may also find it challenging to maintain friendships and relationships with adults.

There are a few things that parents of SEN children can do at home to create a positive and loving environment. To begin, they can devise simple tasks for their children to complete, which will provide them with a sense of accomplishment and pride. Parents should always provide clear and understandable instructions for these tasks. Next, parents can give descriptive praise to their children when they perform well to boost their self-esteem. It is also critical for parents to engage in meaningful conversations with their children and provide a safe space to express their feelings. Finally, parents must recognize that they cannot wholly rely on the school to educate their children. They must do their part by instilling in their children's soft skills that promote self-esteem.

Furthermore, there are several ways that teachers can create a more conducive learning environment for children with SEN. First, teachers must keep their classrooms organized and as free of distractions as possible. It is also critical to plan learning breaks throughout the day. Then, when giving instructions, teachers can incorporate music and voice inflection. Students with special needs may respond better to different voice inflection and tones. When teaching SEN students something new, teachers must be creative with their lesson plans and include multi-sensory visual, auditory, and tactile cues. Last but not the least, teachers must constantly motivate SEN students by complimenting and reassuring them of small achievements.

Children with special needs must not be equated with slow learners or people who are less intelligent. On the contrary, they are frequently as intelligent as their peers; the only difference is that they must learn differently. Teachers and parents should acknowledge that each child has distinct interests, abilities, bits of intelligence, and learning preferences. As a result, ongoing efforts are required to ensure that children with SEN are educated to their full potential.

This effort must be made through special education, defined as educational programs and practices designed for students with learning disabilities and special educational needs. Every child, especially those with special needs, has the right to the same level of education and academic opportunities as their peers. Furthermore, children with special needs will interact with other children, improving their communication and interpersonal skills. Being in a classroom setting will also boost their confidence and self-esteem and create a positive mindset.

WHAT IS THE CURRICULUM FOR SPECIAL EDUCATIONAL NEEDS?

Several international schools have departments dedicated to learning support and assisting students with special needs. Some of the services offered at these schools are as follows:

- Assistance in the classroom

International school teachers work with enrichment coordinators, specialist teachers, and learning support teachers to assist students with numeracy, literacy, and student development.

- One-on-one instruction

Students who require extra attention are taught one-on-one. In addition, some schools provide learning support sessions once or twice a week to assist students in completing schoolwork and extracurricular activities.

- Involvement of parents

International schools with SEN provisions are open to collaborating with parents to develop new ideas and suggestions for accelerating their children's learning.

- Programs with a focus

Specialized programs for students with SEN are available at some international schools. These students will be supported and instructed by specially trained educators and teachers.

- Counseling

Several schools also have an on-site counselor who assists students with academic, emotional, and social issues. If necessary, school counselors can assist students with SEN with personal development and social skill improvement.

DIFFERENT KINDS OF SPECIAL EDUCATIONAL NEEDS

The following are the most common types of learning disorders that children with SEN face:

- Dyslexia

Dyslexia is a language disorder that affects spelling, reading, and comprehension.

- Dyscalculia

Mathematical concepts are complex for children with dyscalculia to grasp. These concepts include numerical organization, quantity comprehension, and calculating value and time.

- Dysgraphia

Dysgraphia is a disorder that affects the physical Act of writing. For example, Dysgraphia affects children who have difficulty holding a pencil and have poor spatial awareness.

- Dyspraxia

Dyspraxia is a condition in which neurological development in muscle coordination and movement is delayed.

- ADHD is an abbreviation for Attention Deficit Hyperactivity Disorder (ADHD)

ADHD is divided into two components: inattentiveness and hyperactivity. Inattentive children have a short attention span, which makes it difficult for them to pay attention and focus on a task.

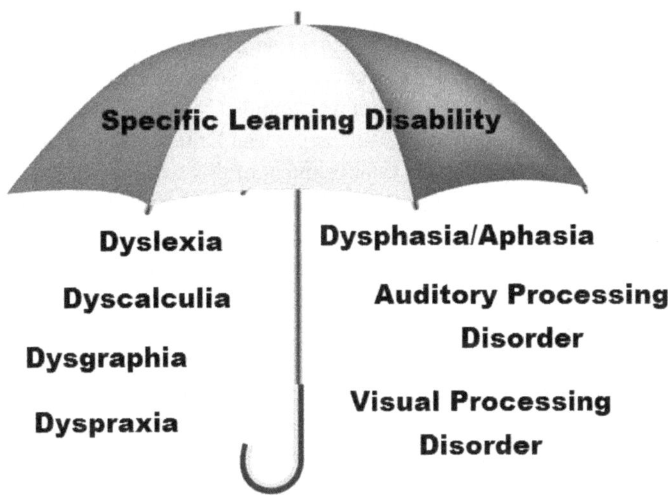

EVOLUTION OF SPECIAL EDUCATION IN MALAYSIA

The development of special education in Malaysia can be divided into four chronological periods: before and during the early colonial period (before 1900), pre-independence (1900–1957), post-independence (1957–1990), and modern Malaysia (1990 to the present).

❖ Before and during the early colonial period (before 1990)

There was no unified education system in Malaysia before and during the early British colonial period (Malaya). Possibly three

There were three types of schools: missionary schools built by British missionary groups, Chinese schools built by local wealthy Chinese communities, and Malay schools (for overviews, refer to Puteh, 2006; Lee,2009). The establishment of these schools, particularly missionary and Chinese schools, was designed for the elite groups. The missionary schools were primarily designed for Royal family relations, wealthy descendants, and those destined for positions in the bureaucracy, whereas the Chinese schools were for wealthy Chinese families who insisted on their Straits-born children learning about their Chinese heritage (Suryadinata, 1997; Tan, Ho & Tan, 2005). These schools did not have the luxury of promoting equal educational opportunities for marginalized people, such as the poor and the disabled, because financial support was heavily reliant on student fees and charitable contributions. In comparison, traditional Malay schools known as *Sekolah Pondok* (shed school) could accept students with disabilities, an old school system implemented in Malaysia's rural areas, emphasizing teaching and learning Islamic values and lifestyles (Salleh, 1981).

❖ Pre-independence (1900–1957)

The first formal special education record in Malaysia dates back to 1948–1950 when the British Strait Government established the Princess Elizabeth Special Education School in Johor Bahru. Personal communication with Ivan Ho, executive director of Malaysia's National Council for the Blind (personal communication, 1 November 2011), yielded information on how the school came. The school was founded by Major Bridges, who became blind during the Myanmar-Japanese war. As the lead British officer in the Malaya Social Welfare Department, he oversaw the establishment of this school with funds raised by British expatriates as a wedding gift for Princess Elizabeth. This school was later given to the Malaysian Association of the Blind before being absorbed into the Ministry of Education (MoE). Before that, non-governmental organizations were primarily responsible for the education of Malaysians with special needs (NGOs). These were consistent with the general trend in the Asia-Pacific region at the time, in which facilities relied almost entirely on the goodwill of NGOs and missionary groups. In Malaysia, one example is the St Nicholas Home for the Blind, which was established in 1926 by Anglican medical missionaries (Jayasooria & Ooi, 1994). Six years after establishing the Princess Elizabeth Special Education School, Penang's first school for students with hearing impairment, known as the Federal School for Deaf Children, was established. Before Malaysia's independence, the Federal Government of Malaya took the first steps in special education to establish these two federal schools. The schools that adopted Braille and sign language curricula based on Western models marked the beginning of Western-initiated influences on the conceptualization of disabilities and special education. Foreign expertise was relied on for knowledge and training during this period. The earliest conceptions used medical and welfare models of provision, resulting in traditional approaches to disabilities that take the biological reality of impairment as their fundamental starting point (Albrecht, Seelman & Bury,2001). The goal of this model is to "care" for people with disabilities by "preventing" and "treating" the functional limitations that come with a disability, whether "mental" or "physical." The emphasis on biomedical definitions of disabilities resulted in a welfare model in policy and practice in which individuals with disabilities were to be 'aided' and 'cared for.' Associated with this model, terms such as *orang kurang upaya* (disabled person) and *orang cacat* (disabled person) were commonly used Malay words to refer to individuals with special needs at the time (Norazit, 2010). Given the emphasis on the functional limitations of people with disabilities, institutionalization and educational exclusion were common practices in Malaysia, as they were in most other countries at the time (Yell, Rogers & Rogers 1998).

- **Post-independence (1957–1990)**

While the Malaysian Federal Government began to integrate special education as a public education component after independence, most early initiatives aimed at students with visual and hearing impairments.

Two notable attempts were the early 1960s implementation of an integration program for these two groups of students and the 1977 establishment of the first boarding school for visually impaired students (Awang Mat, 2001).

Because Malaysia was a new nation, it was natural for them to use a socio-welfare model in their educational planning. Public education was made available to all students, and equal educational opportunities were viewed as critical to maintaining social harmony throughout the population. As a result, the Malaysian government faced a significant challenge in standardizing the diverse school systems established during the British colonial period. The standardization process considered the school curriculum, the languages used, teacher training, and funding sources. Between the 1950s and the 1970s, various policies and acts were put in place to implement large-scale educational reform. The Razak Report 1956, the Education Ordinance 1957, the Abdul Rahman Talib Report 1960, the Education Act 1961, and the Cabinet Report 1974 were enacted (Puteh, 2006). The enforcement and enactment of these acts resulted in Malaysia's current mainstream school systems, including National Schools that implement bilingual policies (Malay and English) and National-type schools that implement a trilingual policy (Malay, English, and a vernacular language, such as Mandarin or Tamil). The unification of Malaysia's disparate school systems necessitated considerable effort and thought from the Ministry of Education during the country's early years of independence. This process took 30 years to produce Malaysia's current mainstream education system.

However, special education planning was compromised, and it was simply not an active process during that period.

Furthermore, the Department of Social Welfare and the Ministry of Health and Social Welfare (now known as the Ministry of Women, Family, and Community Development, MoW) assumed responsibility for most welfare issues affecting people with disabilities.

Representatives from three ministries – the MoE, the MoW, and the MoH (Ministry of Health) – formed a cross-ministerial committee in 1981, which decided that the MoE would be responsible for children with visual impairment, hearing impairment, and mild learning difficulties. The MoW would be responsible for children with physical and moderate to severe mental impairments (Awang Mat, 2001). It was also decided that the Ministry of Health would be in charge of early screening and identifying children born with high-risk conditions. Since then, the Ministry of Education has taken a more active role in special education planning. Among the initiatives taken at this time was the active implementation of integration programs. In Malaysia, an integration program was identified as a special education program in the Education Act of 1986. It was loosely defined as a program for students with special needs, *percantuman di sekolah biasa* (a combined program in mainstream schools). In 1987, all Malaysian states were required to implement an integration program for students with learning disabilities (Awang Mat, 2001). This program represented a 20-year delay in implementing integration programs for students with visual and hearing impairments. During this time (the 1980s to 1990s), teacher education was provided through in-service professional courses and overseas research degrees.

While special education was not a top priority in Malaysia in the middle of this decade, discussion of the topic was informed by rapid development in the United States, the United Kingdom, and other countries that shared philosophical influences with these two countries. The case for an inclusive educational model started to be heard (Lindsay, 2003). The shift in philosophical paradigms in social and educational services from a welfare model to a social model quickly gained worldwide acceptance. This shift has gradually resulted in Asian attitudes toward people with disabilities (Parker, 2001). Disability, according to this model, is the result of an interaction between a person's intrinsic self and the context in which the person performs social roles and activities (Imric, 1996). External social attitudes and policies that have created barriers can explain the inability to perform these roles and activities. This paradigm shift has had a significant impact on Malaysian special education policies in the new millennium.

- **Modern Malaysia (1990 to the present)**

Special education experienced rapid growth during this period.

In 1993, the first pre-service special education teacher preparation program was launched with three universities in the United Kingdom (Jelas & Mohd Ali, 2012), which expanded segregated teacher preparation programs in Malaysia for both mainstream and special educators. Malaysia signed the Salamanca Statement (UNESCO, 1994) in 1994, which advocated for inclusive education for all students. The Special Education Department (now known as the Special Education Division) was established in October 1995 to streamline responsibilities for special education provision. The education went into effect in 1996. This Act included a chapter on special education. For the first time in Malaysian law, "special education" and "special school" were officially defined. The term "special education" was defined as education that meets students' special educational needs, and "special school" was defined as a school that provides special education (according to the rules in Section 41). Students with special needs were classified into three groups: visual impairment, hearing impairment, and learning difficulties (*masalah pembelajaran*). Down syndrome, autistic spectrum disorders (ASD), attention-deficit/hyperactivity disorders (AD/HD), mild mental retardation, and specific learning difficulties (such as dyslexia) are all included in the category of learning difficulties (Ministry of Education Official Portal, 2011). Following this, the Ministry of Education (MoE) issued the Education Rules (Special Education) in 1997. The rules established three special education programs in Malaysian schools: (1) the special school, (2) the integration program, and (3) the inclusive program. The first two programs were a continuation of the MoE's efforts since the pre-and post-independence periods. In terms of inclusive programs, the Ministry of Education announced in 1998 that 53 primary schools and ten secondary schools would participate in an inclusive education program for visually impaired students (Awang Mat, 2001). With this statistic in mind, it is clear that the Ministry defined the resource room placement option in the Least Restrictive Environment (LRE) model (Heward, 2000) as inclusive. Despite Malaysia being a signatory to the Salamanca Statement, policy-making in the 1990s suggested that educational philosophy had not kept pace with the global trend of adopting a more inclusive approach. The special school and the integration program remained the two most prominent placement options for students with special needs. In 2003 and 2008, compulsory education and free education were fully implemented, respectively. Since 2006, all students enrolled in special education programs have received a monthly stipend. In addition, special educators receive a monthly stipend. According to the most recent published figures (Special Education Division, 2009b), there are 28 special primary schools and four special secondary schools, with 2,523 students. According to the most recent MoE records (Ministry of Education, 2008, 2009), there are 1,041 integration programs in primary schools and 55 integration programs for students with visual impairment, hearing impairment, and learning difficulties, totaling 35,639 students. Malaysia's integration program, on the other hand, is still based on the principle of segregation. For example, approximately six students with learning disabilities are placed in a special class attended by special educators in a mainstream school. In general, students learn separately from the other students in the school, except for certain subjects specific to their profile. The level of integration for each student is usually determined by his or her readiness to attend the regular school curriculum and his or her behavioral responses (Lee, 2010). On the other hand, students with visual impairments are enrolled in resource-room-based programs, in which they receive education from mainstream class teachers but are supported by special educators. The Persons with Disabilities (PWD) Act of 2008 mandated improved access to quality education (Government of Malaysia, 2008). The Act represents a paradigm shift from a welfare model to a human rights model that encourages equal and full participation in society. The Act recognizes that people with disabilities should not be excluded from the formal education system because of their disability. However, a major flaw in this Act is that ministries and agencies are not required to comply. There are no provisions for people with disabilities to seek redress when they are discriminated against. There have recently been two new developments in special education provision. The Education (Special Education) Regulations, 2013 (Government of Malaysia, 2013) came into effect in July to replace the 1997 regulations. The government has responded positively to previous criticisms of exclusionary terms (for example, Jelas & Mohd Ali, 2012), as these terms are no longer applicable under the new Regulations. Students with special needs, special education services, and codes of practice are now more detailed, reflecting the field's ongoing maturity. The recently released Preliminary Report of the National Education Blueprint (2013–2025) (Ministry of Education, 2013) also gave special education due to prominence. This roadmap's major thrusts are quality improvement and a commitment to moving students with special needs toward an inclusive education model. These new developments are expected to have a significant impact on special education in the coming years. The state's efforts in policy development and practice did not impede efforts by NGOs to complement or supplement the state's services. Many non-governmental organizations (NGOs) provide early intervention and vocational training for children with specific disabilities, with parents as advocates. However, such a provision does not imply that the NGOs support segregated education. On the contrary, non-governmental organizations (NGOs) have recently called for a more concerted effort to include children with special needs in mainstream schools (Asia Community Service, 2012).

Special Education Program of the Ministry of Education Malaysia

The Ministry of Education (MOE) established the MOE Special Education Program to address the problem of special education students dropping out. The following are some of the educational programmes available:

- **Inclusive Education Program**
- **Special Recovery Program**
- **Integrated Special Education Program (I.S.E.P.) c. (PPKI)**
- **Special Recovery Program (3PK) at the Special Education Service Centre**

I. Special Recovery Program

Since the 1960s, the Ministry of Education Malaysia (MOE) has implemented the Special Recovery Program to assist pupils in primary schools who are having difficulty mastering basic reading, writing, and counting skills (3M).

The Malaysian education system implemented the New Lower School Curriculum (KBSR) in 1983, which focused on mastering fundamental skills. The Special Recovery Program, which has been established in each primary school, is in charge of addressing the issues.

II. Program for Inclusive Education

"Inclusive Education Program" refers to a government or government-aided educational programme for students with special educational needs that includes special needs students as well as other students in the same class.

III. Interdisciplinary Special Education (PPKI)

The Integrated Special Education Program (PPKI) (Merger Plan) was introduced in 1962 for primary school children with disabilities in primary and preventive mainstream curriculums.

1963 - In primary and secondary schools, the Special Education Merger Plan classes for students with hearing impairment begin.

1988 – The Malaysian Ministry of Education launches pioneer classes for underprivileged primary school students with hearing and other learning disabilities across the country.

The program's goals are to:

1. Provide relevant and effective educational access to all Special Needs Students (MBK).

2. Provide opportunities for all MBKs to develop their talents and learning potential through vocational education, resulting in skills that will improve their quality of life.

3. Provide all MBKs with the opportunity to participate in the Early Intervention Program in order to maximise their abilities.

4. Allow MBKs to participate in educational programmes aimed at enhancing existing potential in order to create semi-skilled groups who can then become assets to the country.

5. Potential MBKs should be placed in mainstream classes with other students.

IV. Centre for Special Education Services (3PK)

The Special Education Service Centre (3PK) is a community-based organisation that provides intervention, rehabilitation, and consulting services in the areas of Audiology, Psychology, Language Speech, Occupational Therapy, and Peripatetic.

This center's role and function are to:

1. Implement screening programmes for students with special needs.

2. Use special equipment / standard instruments to conduct tests / assessments to identify specific problems that children and MBKs face.

3. Implementing an intervention/rehabilitation programme for children and MBKs to reduce the impact of disability.

4. Putting in place an early intervention programme that focuses on developmental domains so that these kids are ready for school.

5. To support MBK education as a whole, provide consulting services in the areas of peripatetic, audiology, language speech, occupational therapy, and psychology.

List of support services:

1.Audiology

2. Speech-Language Pathology

3. Peripatetic

4.Occupational Therapy

5. Psychological studies

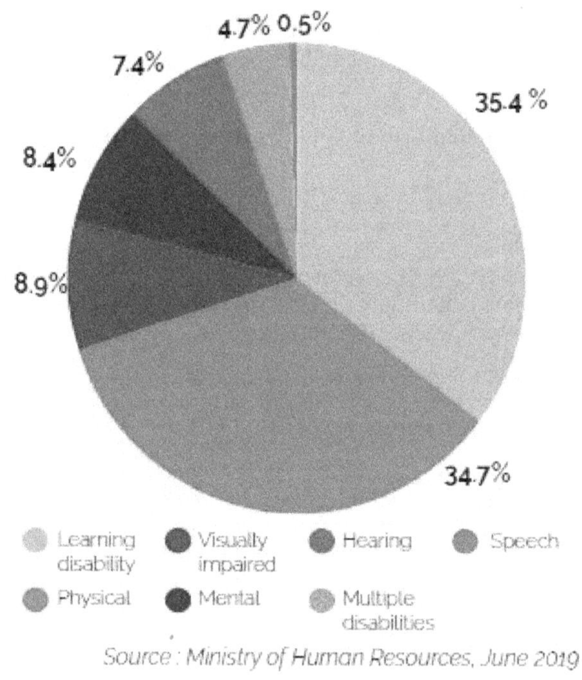

As a result of historical development, there are several important issues today:
The preceding section provided an overview of the changing landscape of special education provision in Malaysia, which was updated in the following section. According to the review findings, much of the progress made has occurred in the last 20 years, particularly since the Special Education Department/Division of the Ministry of Education has taken over planning responsibilities. However, many gaps between policy and practice continue to exist due to an attempt to respond to global trends in special education while also being constrained by local provisions. This section focuses on the most significant issues and dilemmas that have arisen.
Provision of education for students with special needs and making it inclusive

Like other developing countries in the Asia-Pacific region, Malaysia has had to grapple with the establishment of two forms of need within a short period time: the need to provide access to education for children with disabilities and the necessity of making such provision inclusive. This is evident from the review. The authors argue that efforts to provide access to education for children with disabilities and efforts to make special education inclusive necessitate two sets of interconnected skills, particularly in countries where resources and social awareness about inclusion are still limited. According to the authors, this dual challenge continues to make inclusive education a pipe dream for many developing countries. These sets of skills and requirements have now merged into a single set in some Western countries, following a lengthy period of maturation.

In contrast, the transition from a medical model of educational planning to a social model of educational planning has occurred sequentially in the countries designated as "early starters." On the other hand, countries such as Malaysia, which are "late starters," must provide education for children with disabilities and make it inclusive within a short period to keep up with the philosophical shifts that have already occurred. Countries such as Malaysia and other Asia-Pacific nations had some form of the special education system before the philosophical paradigm of inclusion began to take shape, particularly in Malaysia. This means that countries like these have no choice but to maintain two separate educational systems while also attempting to make these two systems as inclusive as possible quickly.
This dual challenge has not been easy. According to the literature, many developing countries in the Asia-Pacific region have had mixed results in balancing the provision of these two necessities at the same time. The situation in Africa, Asian countries, and other developing countries was critically examined by Eleweke and Rodda (2002) nearly a decade ago. They identified three areas of difficulty in the implementation of inclusive education in developing countries, namely: (1) inadequate facilities and personnel training programs, (2) a lack of a funding structure, and (3) a lack of enabling legislation to support inclusive education. Today, these difficulties are still the most significant obstacles that many developing countries, including Malaysia, must overcome (Lee & Low, 2013). As a result, many low-income and developing countries have adopted a more pragmatic approach to service delivery known as the "twin-track" approach (Bines & Lei, 2011; Croft, 2012). With the advancement of the so-called "twin-track" approach, we can demonstrate that the provision of inclusive education requires a different set of resources and skills than the traditional educational model. It has been suggested that the "twin-track approach" may be appropriate until more support for inclusive practice is available, as Bines and Lei (2011) have pointed out.
Encouragement of diversity within a highly structured education system

Even though Malaysia has undergone active revision of educational legislation over the past ten years, the pace of change has been deemed slow in the country (Ministry of Education,2008, 2009). This observation suggests gaps in the transference of policies into practice, which can be traced back to the roots of Asian values in the educational systems in which they were developed. A high degree of centralization characterizes the Malaysian education system, with policies dictated at the federal level, as with other Asian systems (Ratnavadivel, 1999). In practice, this centralised structure manifests itself in a traditional didactic teaching methodology that emphasizes excellence in examinations as the dominant ideology of educational effectiveness (Corbett, 1999). An education system with such a high degree of structure may not encourage learners to be diverse. Students with learning difficulties are not as readily accepted into the mainstream as students with visual impairment, owing to their lower levels of academic achievement.

Furthermore, teacher efforts to include students with special needs are not recognized, as was demonstrated in a study on "unconscious inclusion" (Lee & Low, 2013); instead, teachers are held accountable for the poor examination results obtained by their students with special educational needs. Instead of rewarding schools based on their performance in examinations, as is currently the case, the government could establish an alternative reward system to recognize schools for their efforts to include students with special needs (Asia Community Service, 2012). As an alternative to placing students in special classes to avoid examinations, testing accommodations and alternative assessment systems for students with special needs should be given due consideration instead.

The significance of financial support

Despite the emphasis placed on an inclusive education model in the new acts, many budgets and resources are still allocated to special schools and integration programs (Ministry of Education, 2008; Ministry of Education, 2009; Government of Malaysia, 2008). RM236 million was spent on upgrading special schools and the construction of new vocational special schools during the Ninth Malaysia Plan budget allocations (Ministry of Education, 2009); RM40 million was spent on upgrading integration programs in mainstream schools, and another RM10 million was spent on upgrading special education pre-school programs. In contrast, there was no official record of any budget allocation to promote inclusive education. This represents a significant misalignment between policy formulation and policy implementation. It has already been mentioned that countries such as Malaysia must deal with the dual challenge of developing special education while also working to make it more inclusive at the same time. Malaysia's emphasis on developing special education provisions, rather than the idea of making special education inclusive, is reflected in the budget allocation. However, with the new emphasis on inclusion in the National Education Blueprint (2013–2025), positive changes in the direction of inclusive education funding are expected to take place shortly. Restructuring pre-service teacher preparation

Currently, there are separate teacher preparation programs for special education and mainstream education, which do not promote inclusivity in the classroom. This lack of dynamic collaboration between mainstream and special educators has been highlighted by Jelas (2000) and Lee (2010). They both argue that a unified approach to teacher training is required to address this issue. Students with special needs will then have the advantage of teachers who are familiar with the requirements of both systems and, as a result, will be better prepared to plan for the inclusion of all students in the classroom. In response to this need, the state has established a target for all teachers to receive basic special needs education training during the second wave of implementation (2016–2020) as part of the National Education Blueprint. Multidisciplinary support and collaboration

In special education, a multidisciplinary team approach has been adopted around the world to use the expertise of professionals from various disciplines. Using the currently advocated working model, Malaysia has been implementing it since 1981, with the restructuring of policies and division of ministry responsibility to improve service delivery efficiency. However, what is lacking is the integration of these services to provide support to students with disabilities and special educational requirements. A multidisciplinary approach necessitates strong, ongoing collaboration across agencies; however, this collaboration appears to be lacking in Malaysia at the moment. As a result, fragmented service provision has become a common phenomenon, with students and their families struggling to cope with the dispersion of support services across ministries. Parents must deal with three different ministries on their own time and initiative. Case referral across settings and individual progress monitoring can be made more efficient by utilizing a middle agent who serves in the capacity of a case manager.

Furthermore, some international structures (for example, Klein & Harris, 2004) employ itinerant consultants who travel between locations to monitor the progress of individual cases and assist individuals and their families in collaborating with the various health, social, and educational personnel involved. This is something that Malaysia could learn from in the future. Provision of related services

The Special Educational Division of the Ministry of Education (MoE) has established Special Education Service Centres throughout Malaysia to bring related services, such as audiology and speech therapy, into special and mainstream schools. However, their availability remains limited due to a lack of staff positions created specifically for these services. There has been significant resistance to the full implementation of inclusive education in Malaysia due to a scarcity of allied health support services in schools. Program outcomes

Another shortcoming identified in the provision of special education in Malaysia is the absence of a mechanism for evaluating the program's outcomes. This shortcoming exists both at the individual case level and the level of program implementation. Information on the various programs organized by the Ministry of Education to improve the quality of special education and expand current provision can be found in the Ministry of Education's National Report for 2009. (Ministry of Education, 2009). These programs include the Outreach program, running since 2005, and some pilot projects on inclusive education for students with autism spectrum disorder (ASD) (Hussin, Quek & Loh, 2008; Hussin, Loh & Quek, 2008). However, again, no outcome measure appears to be beneficial.

Childhood education and the development of children's cognitive and psychological abilities

Education is one of the most important pillars of a successful life. The quality and versatility of the type of education a person receives from the beginning has a significant impact on his or her cognitive development, psychological development, and personality development. It provides a strategic and valuable insight into how to shape the cognitive and overall development of children, which begins as early as elementary school. The skills and learnings that are instilled in children through education, academics, and a variety of other procedures can be valuable in the development of a person into a fully developed human being in the future. As a result, selecting the most appropriate school for your children's education is critical, beginning with their early childhood years.

Childhood Education is divided into several segments

The early childhood education stage is defined as the period between the ages of 0 and 8 years old.

Childhood education in the middle childhood stage is considered to be between the ages of 8 and 12 years old.

Children between the ages of 12 and 18 years old are considered to be in the adolescence childhood stage of education.

Early childhood is considered to be the most critical period in a child's development. The United Nations Educational, Scientific, and Cultural Organization (UNESCO) refers to this as a "smooth transition" from prenatal care to primary school. This concept has its origins in the European Union countries. This is the age group that experiences the most rapid cognitive development. The nervous system, which is made up of neurons, brain cells, and other developments, develops at a rapid pace. From this point on, the ability to comprehend, perceive, and reciprocate is established. Education at this level allows children to learn from a wide range of sources of information. It aids in the development of self-esteem, confidence, and the ability to set perspective, as well as the gradual development of the personality. It is more about learning mainstream academics than anything else; it teaches through insight and imagination rather than anything else. The development of cognitive and psychological development occurs at this level of education.

Mentally preparing oneself to shape one's personality

In the modern era, the educational system is structured in a very systematic manner in order to shape career paths, promote cognitive development, and improve children's

overall abilities. Children are given the best possible foundation for growth and development when data, facts, and figures are organised in a systematic manner. In this case, the strategy and mechanism demonstrate how to apply data and theory to real-world situations.

For example, a child may engage in play with items that are not readily available in real life. In any case, they consider it to be true and proceed with the performance. Frequently, we find children pretending to be in the kitchen, believing it to be real. However, the food and vegetables are a far cry from what they should be. This ability to imagine allows them to perceive a life of action in the kitchen that is synchronised with the kitchen's real-life activities. In Montessori schools, we frequently find such intuitive games as well as an educational system that successfully integrates children into real life by acting as a bridge between the two.

Education has an impact on the psychological verticals that exist.

The following are the five major verticals that education has an impact on in terms of psychology:

- **Behaviourism**
- **Cognitivism**
- **Constructivism**
- **Experientialism**
- **Theories of social and contextual learning**

The study module taught at school and by academics has a systematic impact on all of these factors, resulting in an individual who is mentally healthy and full of confidence and self-esteem. A sound psychological foundation is essential for living a successful life.

What is the most important thing to remember? Education contributes to the development of cognitive abilities.

Education contributes to the development of the eight most important cognitive abilities. Developing the ability to perceive any matter by listening, thinking about, and looking at it is what sustained attention is all about. Overall, the process can be characterised as one of paying attention. It is the most fundamental ability to comprehend any subject.

The process of inhibiting responses to distraction-inducing impulses is referred to as response inhibition. Some people are able to recognise the importance of the task and resist the temptation to become distracted, whereas others are unable to resist the temptation and become distracted.

The process of receiving incoming information and putting it into action within a specified period of time is referred to as speed of processing information. This is an important component of one's intelligence quotient. Those who suffer from attention deficits will be unable to achieve a high level of information processing.

In order to achieve success, one must have cognitive flexibility on multiple levels. Because it alters the perspective of what you think, how you think, and how long you can maintain attention, it allows the brain to mould to the thought procedure.

A person's ability to multitask and distribute their attention among a variety of tasks at the same time is referred to as simultaneity of attention. Sustained attention, response inhibition, and speeding up the information process are all combined in a consolidated form known as strategic planning.

Memory – It refers to the ability to recall information, perceive information, and perform the required task under given circumstances. Working memory is a more developed form of working memory, in which we keep things like a sketch pad.

Information, concepts, and skills are organised into specific categories in a systematic manner to form a cognitive foundation for application, analysis, and evaluation of the newly acquired knowledge or concept. The category serves as the foundation for both language and formulation.

Recognition of patterns – Inductive thinking, also known as pattern recognition, is a remarkable ability of the brain to deduce logic and then create classification patterns as a result of this deduction. This aids in determining what is going to happen in the next scene. It serves as the foundation for all scientific inquiry and resolution.

Training in the classroom and the academic process

Teachers design their classroom instruction and academic structure to encourage the development and maintenance of these cognitive skills in students. A person is gradually introduced to, trained in, and skilled in the structure of psychological and cognitive skill sets as a result of exposure to a variety of subjects and their rearing structure.

Improvements in the Learning Procedure

The academic structure in school is designed in such a way that students can develop mental capability while training on a tried-and-true foundation. Due to the fact that they are from playgroups, students are guided through structured training procedures. There are several instructional procedures that are used to evaluate the learning abilities of different individuals. It alters an individual's behaviour in a desired direction while they are in a controlled environment between two controlled environments. It establishes a logical link between educational attainment and psychological behaviour in a connecting environment.

PIAGET'S STAGES OF COGNITIVE DEVELOPMENT

As identified by Piaget's Theory of Cognitive Development (1970), there are four major stages through which children progress: sensorimotor, pre-operational, concrete-operational, and formal-operational stages. In accordance with this theory, these stages reflect differences in a child's cognitive abilities, and key cognitive tasks cannot be taught to learners until they have reached a specific stage of cognitive development.

- **The Sensorimotor Stage**

Ages: From birth to 2 years

- **We are in the Sensorimotor Stage of development from birth to two years of age.**
- **The Most Important Characteristics and Shifts in Development: By observing their movements and sensations, the infant learns about the world.**
- **Sucking, grasping, looking, and listening are all basic actions that help children learn about the world around them.**
- **Children learn that things exist even when they are not visible to the naked eye (object permanence), and that they exist as separate entities from the people and objects in their immediate surroundings." They are aware that their actions have the potential to cause events in the world.**

❖ The Preoperational Stage

Ages: 2 to 7 Years

- Major Characteristics and Developmental Changes: Children start thinking symbolically and learn to represent objects with words and pictures.
- At this age, children are egocentric and have difficulty seeing things from other people's perspectives.
- While they are improving their language and thinking skills, they still have a tendency to think in very concrete terms.

❖ The Concrete Operational Stage

Ages: 7 to 11 Years

- Major Characteristics and Changes in Development
- Children begin to think logically about concrete events during this stage.
- They start to grasp the concept of conservation, such as the fact that the amount of liquid in a short, wide cup is equal to the amount in a tall, skinny glass.
- Their reasoning becomes more logical and organised, but their thinking remains very concrete.
- Inductive logic, or reasoning from specific information to a general principle, is taught to children at an early age.

❖ The Formal Operational Stage

Ages: 12 and Up

- The adolescent or young adult begins to think abstractly and reason about hypothetical problems at this stage.
- The concept of abstraction emerges.
- Teenagers begin to consider moral, philosophical, ethical, social, and political issues that necessitate the use of theoretical and abstract reasoning.

- Begin to apply deductive logic, which is the process of reasoning from a general principle to specific data.

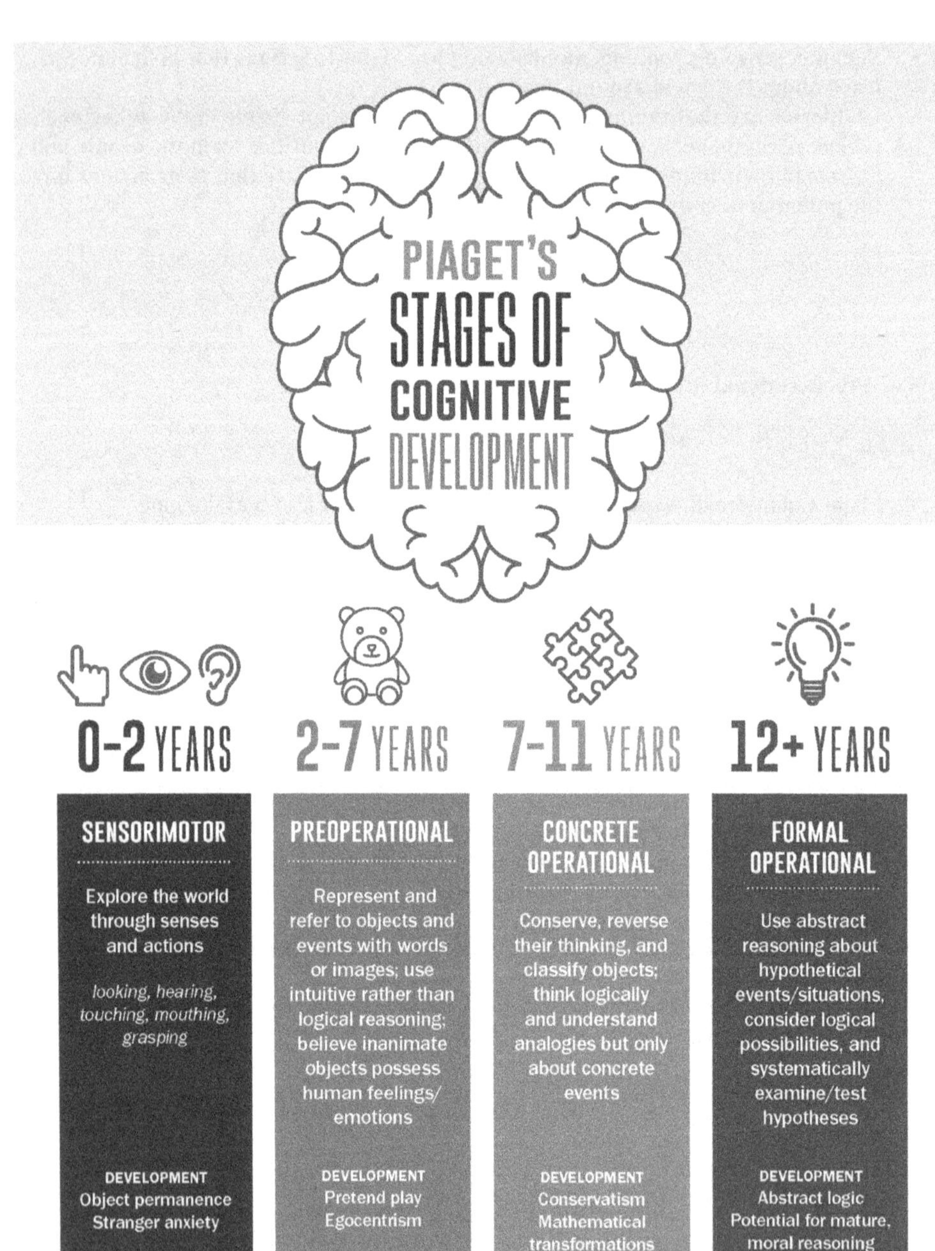

Research and practise conducted over several decades has produced substantial changes in the way students with learning disabilities are supported in schools throughout the United States and other countries. For example, federal policy defines various categories of disabilities that may entitle students to receive special education services or other educational accommodations in the United States of America. The Individuals with Disabilities Education Act (IDEA) categorises a variety of disabilities, some of which create barriers to educational opportunities or restrict students' ability to participate in certain activities. Deafness, blindness, and orthopaedic disabilities are examples of such conditions. When the learning mechanisms of the brain are still intact and functioning normally, these types of disabilities may still be present and manifest themselves.

Other disabilities, on the other hand, are directly related to the brain's learning processes. Specific learning disabilities are defined as deficits in the underlying psychological processes that are involved in the process of learning new information. Such deficits may have an impact on visual working memory, verbal working memory, processing speed, short-term memory, and other cognitive processes, among other things. Intellectual disability also has a direct impact on the brain's ability to learn new things. Other disabilities that have been identified include underdeveloped cognitive processes, to name a few. For example, students with autism spectrum disorder (ASD) or attention deficit hyperactivity disorder (ADHD) typically have difficulties with attention, working memory, and other executive functions, all of which are critical for learning.

To assist students receiving special education services, educators who work with students who have deficits in underlying cognitive processes that interfere with their ability to learn to read, write, and do math typically use three categories of strategies: reading, writing, and mathematics.

It is critical to recognise that the goal of these strategies is to circumvent the cognitive processes that are weak in order to reduce the severity of the effects of processing deficits on the individual. When teaching a student who has limited working memory capacity and who is unable to remember a set of three instructions, the teacher would eliminate the need for the student to hold three items of information in working memory and would instead give the instructions one at a time. That is an example of a negotiated settlement. These commonly employed intervention strategies frequently fail

to produce positive outcomes for students. The academic achievement of students receiving special education services continues to lag behind the general population, and they frequently rely on these services throughout their educational careers. According to recent research, the ineffectiveness of these strategies can be attributed to significant cognitive deficits in the students, which are preventing them from making progress in their learning.

Recently, researchers and educators have begun to investigate a fourth strategy, which is the remediation of cognitive processes that have been identified as being weak. The idea is that by assisting students in developing weak cognitive areas, they will be able to learn more like their typically developing peers, rather than working around them or employing strategies to get around their cognitive weaknesses. Several research efforts have concentrated on the training of working memory, a cognitive skill also known as an executive function, which has been shown to be highly correlated with a variety of aspects of academic achievement. Many studies have demonstrated that training improves working memory, but not all of these studies have demonstrated that the benefits of training are transferred to academic performance.

Both cognitive and academic gains have been achieved.

Roles and Responsibilities of the Special Education Teacher

A special educator works with children who have a variety of disabilities and is responsible for their educational needs. In addition, these children's educational experiences will necessitate a variety of services, modifications, and accommodations. If you plan to work in the field of special education or are already working in it, you must have a thorough understanding of each type of disability and the unique needs of children with that disability.

The Individuals with Disabilities Education Act of 2004 clearly defines the various types of disabilities.

Autism, deaf-blindness, emotional disturbance, hearing impairment (including deafness), mental retardation, multiple disabilities, orthopaedic impairment, other health impairment, specific learning disability, speech or language impairment, traumatic brain injury, or visual impairment are examples of these conditions (including blindness).

In today's schools, special education teachers play a critical role in the proper education of exceptional students. The teacher is unique in that he or she can fulfil a variety of roles in the educational setting. Each of these distinct roles, however, has a different set of responsibilities and functions. Understanding these responsibilities will only help the special educator gain a better understanding of the role and improve their chances of success.

1- A general education teacher in a self-contained special education classroom: This position would entail working in a special education setting with a group of disabled students. When a student is ready for mainstreaming, which involves placing a disabled child in a general education classroom for a portion of the school day, this type of setting allows for the use of mainstreaming as an educational tool. A teaching assistant usually assists the teacher in a self-contained classroom. In this type of setting, the special educator may be responsible for a variety of tasks, including but not limited to: * Curriculum development * Parent conferences * Group standardised tests for pre- and post-testing * Participation in the annual review, which is a meeting held by the IEP Committee each year to discuss the progress of each child with a disability and to plan the Individual Education Plan for the following year. * Participation in the triennial evaluation process, which occurs every three years to determine if the original classification's conditions are still present or need to be modified. The requirement in this case would be limited to annual progress reports and recommendations. * Maintaining a close eye on the IEP, modifications, and accommodations

2- In a categorical or noncategorical resource room, the resource teacher: A categorical resource room is a resource room in a special school that deals with only one type of exceptionality. A non categorical resource room is a resource room that is usually found in a regular mainstream school and is used to educate children with a variety of special needs at the same time. Close collaboration with each child's homeroom teacher is required, as is the transfer of practical techniques and suggestions to aid the child's success in the general education setting. In this type of setting, the special educator may be responsible for a variety of tasks, including but not limited to:

Curriculum modification: In this case, the resource teacher works with the classroom teacher to adapt the curriculum to the child's learning style and needs. * Meetings with parents * Educational evaluator: The resource room teacher is frequently asked to conduct educational evaluations for initial, screening, and triennial assessments. * Group standardised tests for pre- and post-testing * Participation in the annual review, which is a meeting held by the IEP Committee each year to discuss the progress of each child with a disability and to plan the Individual Education Plan for the following year. * Participation in the triennial evaluation process, which occurs every three years to determine if the original classification's conditions are still present or need to be modified. The requirement would be either to discuss test results or to provide an update on the student's progress and recommendations for the following year. * Monitoring the IEP, modifications, and accommodations

3- A member of the Child Study Team (CST) who is an educational evaluator: The CST is a school-based support group that meets to discuss and make recommendations for high-risk students. A complete and professional understanding of testing and evaluation procedures, as well as diagnosis and interpretation of test results, is required of an educational evaluator on this team. In this type of setting, the special educator may be responsible for a variety of tasks, including but not limited to: * Educational evaluator for preliminary assessments (evaluations performed on students being classified for the first time). * Participation in the triennial evaluation process, which occurs every three years to determine if the conditions for the original classification are still present or need to be modified.

4-A member of the IEP Committee (also known as the Committee on Special Education or IEP Committee depending on the state): The IEP Committee is a district-based committee mandated by federal law with the responsibility of classifying, placing, and evaluating all disabled children in the district. Interpreting educational test results, making recommendations, and diagnosing strengths and weaknesses for the Individual Educational Plan, a list of goals, needs, and objectives required for every disabled student, are all part of this role. In this type of setting, the special educator may be responsible for a variety of tasks, including but not limited to: * interpreting educational test results, * recommending IEP Committee, IEP, classification, or placement * determining strengths and weaknesses in order to create an Individual Educational Plan (a list of goals , needs and objectives required for every disabled student)

5-A member of a multidisciplinary teaching team in a departmentalized programme educating secondary students: This is a relatively new programme in secondary schools, in which students with disabilities follow a departmentalized programme like other students, but special education teachers teach all of their classes. In this type of setting, the special educator may be responsible for a variety of tasks, including but not limited to: * Curriculum development * Parent conferences * Participation in the annual review—an annual meeting held by the IEP Committee to discuss the progress of each child with a disability and plan the following year's Individual Education Plan * Participation in the triennial evaluation process—a three-year evaluation to determine if the conditions for the original classification are still in place The requirement in this case would be limited to annual progress reports and recommendations. * IEP monitoring, modifications, and accommodations

6-A consultant teacher: A consultant teacher is a special education teacher who is assigned to work with a disabled child in a mainstreamed classroom. The IEP Committee may decide that it is in the child's best interests to receive services in his or her own classroom rather than leaving to attend a pull-out programme such as a resource room. This can happen if a child has fragmentation issues, in which case the schedule may force him or her to leave the classroom in the middle of one lesson to go to the resource room and then return in the middle of another. For some children, this fragmentation can be extremely confusing. In this type of setting, the special educator may be responsible for a variety of tasks, including but not limited to: * Curriculum modification: the consultant teacher works with the classroom teacher to adapt the curriculum to the child's learning style and needs. * Parent conferences * Pre- and post-testing using group standardised tests * Participation in the annual review—an annual meeting held by the IEP Committee to discuss the progress of each child with a disability and to plan the next year's Individual Education Plan * Participation in the triennial evaluation process—a three-year evaluation to determine if the original classification conditions are still present or need to be modified. The requirement would be either to discuss test results or to provide an update on the student's progress and recommendations for the following year. * Maintaining a close eye on the IEP, modifications, and accommodations

7- An itinerant teacher: An itinerant teacher is a special education teacher who is hired by a company to travel to different schools in different districts and work with children with disabilities. This ensures that each child receives the necessary auxiliary services and allows a district to meet requirements without having to develop its own programme. In this type of setting, the special educator may be responsible for a variety of tasks, including but not limited to:

* Curriculum modification: in this case, the itinerant teacher works with the classroom teacher to adapt the curriculum to the child's learning style and needs. * Meetings with parents * Educational evaluator: the itinerant room teacher may be asked to conduct educational evaluations in some cases. The district will usually pay the agency a fee for this service if this is the case. * Group standardised tests for pre- and post-testing * Participation in the annual review, which is a meeting held by the IEP Committee each year to discuss the progress of each child with a disability and to plan the Individual Education Plan for the following year. * Participation in the triennial evaluation process, which occurs every three years to determine if the original classification's conditions are still present or need to be modified. The requirement would be either to discuss test results or to provide an update on

the student's progress and recommendations for the following year. * Maintaining a close eye on the IEP, modifications, and accommodations

8-An Inclusion Teacher who works in either a partial or full inclusion programme.

A mainstream class with a population of children with and without disabilities is known as an inclusion class. A general education teacher and a special education teacher will work together in this classroom. In this type of setting, the special educator may be responsible for a variety of tasks, including but not limited to: * Curriculum development and modification: the special education teacher works with the classroom teacher to develop and modify the curriculum to meet the learning styles and needs of the students with disabilities. * Student assistance: During a lesson, a special education teacher may circulate among the disabled students to ensure that they understand the concepts being taught, assist with note-taking skills, answer questions, and reinforce concepts.

Conferences with parents * Group standardised tests for pre- and post-testing * Participation in the annual review, which is a meeting held by the IEP Committee each year to discuss the progress of each child with a disability and to plan the Individual Education Plan for the following year. * Participation in the triennial evaluation process, which occurs every three years to determine if the original classification's conditions are still present or need to be modified. The requirement would be either to discuss test results or to provide an update on the student's progress and recommendations for the following year. * Maintaining a close eye on the IEP, modifications, and accommodations 9-A teacher in a special school's self-contained special education classroom: This position would entail working in a special education setting with a group of more severely disabled students. Because of the severity of the disabilities displayed by this population of students, the teacher in this setting is usually assisted by a teaching assistant as well as aides. In this type of setting, the special educator may be responsible for a variety of tasks, including but not limited to: * Parent conferences * Curriculum development * Group standardised tests for pre- and post-testing * Participation in the annual review, which is a meeting held by the IEP Committee each year to discuss the progress of each child with a disability and to plan the Individual Education Plan for the following year. * Participation in the triennial evaluation process, which occurs every three years to determine if the original classification's conditions are still present or need to be modified. The requirement in this case would be limited to annual progress reports and recommendations. * Maintaining a close eye on the IEP, modifications, and accommodations * If in secondary school, working closely with related service providers, particularly vocational and transition specialists.

In addition to the services provided by the district, the special education teacher provides evaluation and remediation services for children with disabilities. In this type of setting, the special educator may be responsible for a variety of tasks, including but not limited to: * Curriculum modification suggestions to the district: Here, the private practitioner assists the classroom teacher in making curriculum modifications to meet the learning style and needs of the child with a disability. * Participation in the annual review—an annual meeting held by the IEP Committee to discuss the progress of each child with a disability and to plan the next year's Individual Education Plan * Participation in the triennial evaluation process—a three-year evaluation to determine if the conditions for the original classification are still met. The requirement would be either to discuss test results or to provide an update on the student's progress and recommendations for the following year. Whatever role one plays, they will be confronted with a variety of situations that will necessitate practical decisions and relevant recommendations. Whatever role one plays in special education, they must be able to fully comprehend symptoms, causality, evaluation, diagnosis, prescription, and remediation, as well as effectively communicate vital information to professionals, parents, and students. Without a doubt, they will need to learn a lot, have a strong legal and educational foundation, and be prepared for an exciting, rewarding, but demanding career.

Reference: AASEP's Staff Development Course–Roles and Responsibilities of the Special Education Teacher – Copyright AASEP (2006)

Parent's role in special education process

Parents, like school personnel, are full and equal members of the IEP team. Parents are valuable team members because they have firsthand knowledge of their child's abilities and needs. Parents have the right to attend meetings regarding their children's identification, evaluation, development of IEPs, and educational placement. They, like all members of the IEP team, have the right to ask questions, dispute points, and request plan changes.

An IEP meeting is not the same as a Parent/Teacher conference, in which the parent converses with the teacher and receives progress and performance reports on the student. In order to fully participate in developing their child's IEP, parents must be knowledgeable about their child's specific disabilities, their rights under federal and state law, and the policies and procedures of the local education agency (LEA). Many parents are unaware of this information when their child is first diagnosed with a disability. Some centres may also send a knowledgeable individual to accompany a parent to IEP meetings to assist the parent in participating more fully in the process.

Parents and guardians are the only people who truly understand their children's physical, social, developmental, and family histories.

While they may not be educators, parents are the only adults in the educational process who have been and will continue to be deeply involved throughout their child's school career; and while they may not be educators, they bring their years of experience in other professions and aspects of life to the process.

While children spend approximately six hours per day at school, they only receive a few minutes of a teacher's undivided attention in a classroom. Parents can work side by side with their children on homework and other learning activities for extended periods of time. Parents may be the only adults who pay attention to their children's work and solicit feedback from them. As a result, no one else in the meeting has the perspective of a parent.

No one is more invested in and motivated to see their child succeed and thrive than their own parents, and this alone makes the parent an important member of the IEP team.

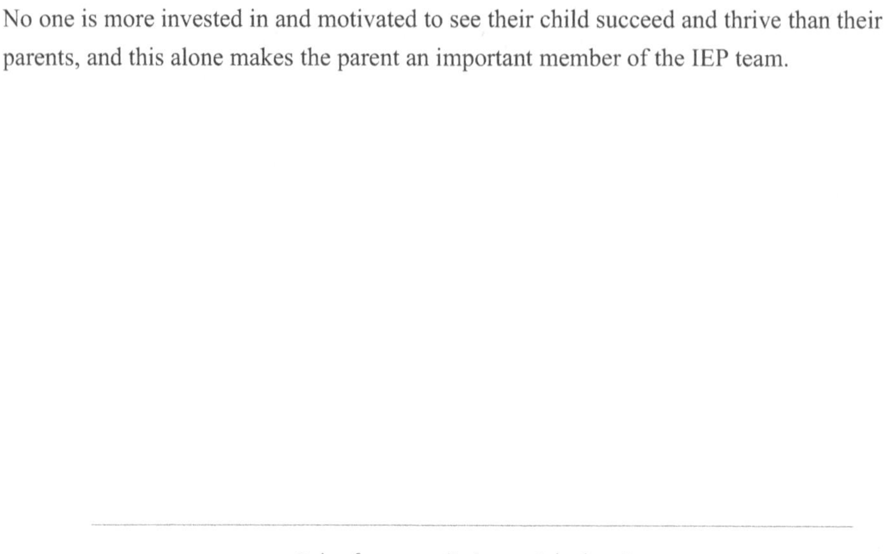

Role of community in special education

Although having the right people at the table is important, it is not so much who is involved in the community of care for students with disabilities and their families as it is how they are involved. We can gain insight into the critical components of an effective community of care by looking at the family-centered practises that are considered a practice-of-choice in early intervention. Family-centered practises are distinguished by the treatment of families with dignity and respect, the sharing of information so that families and students can make informed decisions, and the availability of options for involvement in the provision of services (Dunst, Trivette, & Hamby, 2006). Most school teams believe they treat families with respect and provide them with information to help them make decisions, but the reality is that the manner in which they achieve those goals is frequently perceived very differently by families. According to Dunst et al. (2006), a practice-based theory of family-centered help includes relational and participatory practises. Active listening, compassion, empathy, and respect are examples of relational practises. Participatory practises are defined as "individualised, flexible, and responsive to family concerns and priorities, as well as involving informed choices and family involvement in achieving desired goals and outcomes" (Dunst, Trivette, & Hamby, 2007, p. 371). Participatory practise stands out as the most distinct of the two. Listening well, demonstrating empathy, and being "nice" are all important, but families notice a difference when the service remains professional-centered despite these factors (Espe-Sherwindt, 2008). Community is frequently viewed as a physical concept, requiring the physical gathering of people in time and space. In this chapter, we argue that community is more usefully conceived of as a mode of thought, an orientation. When teachers see parents as resources, doors open to them that can help make their job easier. They can reach out to parents in a new way, one that is truly collaborative and based on mutual assistance. When parents assist teachers in making their jobs easier, and teachers assist parents in making their jobs easier, the benefits to the student are enormous. Family therapists, who have been trained to see how people make sense of their worlds, themselves, and their problems, can assist parents and teachers in making better sense, having clearer understandings of a student's behaviours and failures, and acting as translators of seemingly nonsensical behaviour. When teachers recognise that working with parents in a family-centered, rather than a professional-centered, manner can help them provide a higher quality service, the spirit of the 2004 IDEA is realised, and a true special education community emerges.

Reference : Kate Warner Karla Hull Martha Laughlin . "The Role of Community in Special Education: A Relational Approach" In Interdisciplinary Connections to Special Education: Important Aspects to Consider

Problems faced during the Pandemic in relation to Special Needs Education

Although the Ministry of National Education took some precautions after the outbreak to prevent course losses, it also took some bold decisions at the primary level, launching distance education applications with the help of volunteer teachers. Despite the lack of an open education practises policy in the educational system, all levels of education are focusing on the potential of remote learning. However, because there is no local action plan in place, all institutions, including individual teachers, are looking for ways to improve the recovery mode of action for lost classes. Zoom has ideally become an alternative platform for proposing interaction between students and teachers, as well as fostering meetings among colleagues and enriching collegiality (Huang, et al, 2020). Because this study is based on Gilly Salmon's Carpe Diem model, which challenges collaboration and a well-planned course of action, it emphasises the importance of local action. There is a regional plan as well as a specific action plan for those with special needs. Giving those students the opportunity to learn and teach is not enough; family education must also be supported during the pandemic. As a result, during a pandemic, leadership and the proper selection of enabling technology are critical. Teachers have taken the initiative in this period to find ways to communicate with and reach out to students. Teachers prepared presentations on the computer using the "zoom" programme for these distance education applications, and students with the appropriate conditions and environments began to watch the applications appropriate for their age levels and then began to solve questions about the subjects. Individuals who require special education should be educated differently than their peers for a variety of reasons, including developmental characteristics (Eurybase, 2009; Altnay, Altnay, Dagli, and Altnay, 2018). Because learning facilitation differs in special education, distance learning can be considered as an alternative in this epidemic process for students whose development levels fluctuate according to their age group. However, special training should be provided for students with special needs who have different levels of development than the general population (Elikten, 2018). If accessible technologies and information are provided, distance education has the potential to support special needs students' learning. In these students, special education practises become more important. Special education refers to the education provided to students who have developmental characteristics that set them apart from their peers. Based on this point, the goal of this study is to answer the questions of what is done in distance education and how students can benefit from it, so that special education students in primary schools can continue their education during the epidemic (Zhang, et al., 2020).

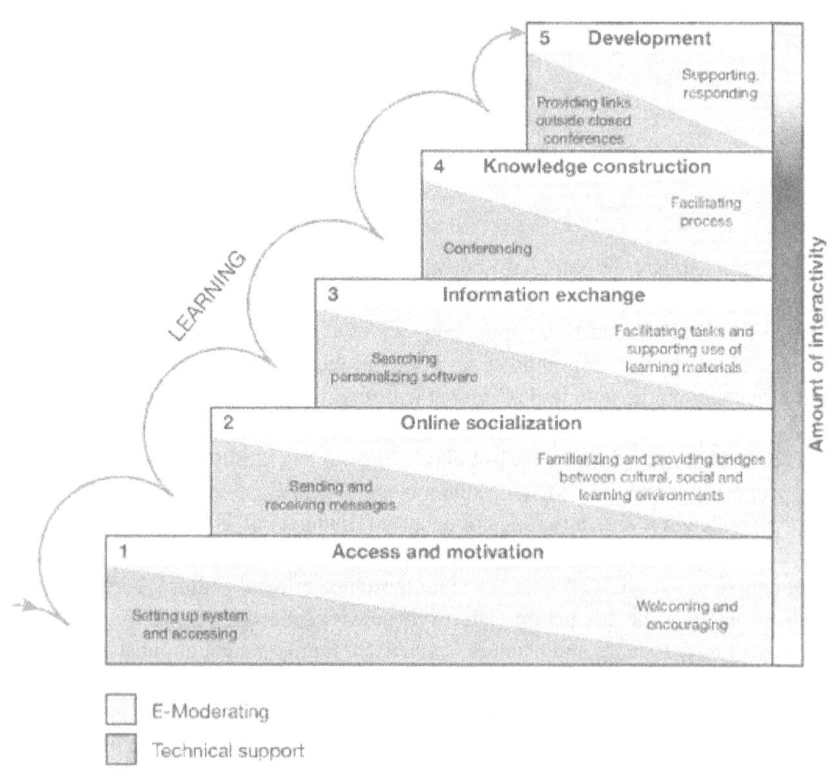

Gilly Salmon's Carpe Diem Model

In the presence or absence of the pandemic, children with disabilities are among the world's most vulnerable, stigmatised, and marginalised groups of people (UNICEF, n.d.). The closure of schools as a result of the COVID-19 pandemic has impacted special needs students significantly. Children with disabilities such as vision, hearing, or cognitive functioning, according to Prior (2020), are unable to access information on COVID-19, including preventive measures. The closure of schools and the implementation of social distancing protocols have thrown children with disabilities' daily routines into disarray. In-person learning suspension has also denied special needs children access to important learning tools and resources; modifications and adaptive equipment and services installed in the school to help special needs children learn may not be available at home. Learners must have access to necessary technological resources such as the internet and assistive devices in order for home-based distance learning to be successful. Unfortunately, the lack of these resources has had an impact on continuous learning at home. 11 Adaptation of Learners as a Result of the Impact Children with disabilities have a hard time adjusting to online learning platforms. For example, the incompatibility of assistive devices with online learning platforms makes it difficult for students with visual and hearing disabilities to learn effectively from home. The closure of schools due to the COVID-19 pandemic has harmed the development of social skills, interactional behaviour, and psychomotor skills among students with ASD, according to Asbury et al. (2020). Their usual learning routine has been disrupted by the shift to online learning. Due to the disruption of their daily routines and inability to participate in outdoor activities as a result of the social distancing protocol, their development has deteriorated (Stenhoff et al., 2020). According to the authors, children with ASD are more agitated, anxious, and grumpy. When their routines are disrupted or they are faced with uncertainty, many of them develop unpleasant developmental behaviours. Deficiency in Infrastructure During the Covid-19 pandemic, special needs children felt more helpless and frustrated due to a lack of physical infrastructure, assistive technology, inclusive education, and confinement at home. Children with developmental and intellectual delays, according to Asbury et al. (2020), have difficulty understanding social distancing and its impact during the pandemic. The majority of special needs children are unable to comprehend what covid-19 is and the precautions that must be taken to avoid it, including the pandemic's hygiene regulations. For students with special needs, ineffective instruction methods, a lack of progress, learning, therapy, and students' inability to participate have become a challenge. It's been difficult to reimagine home as a school because these students understand that a home is a place for relaxation, socialisation, and family time. 12 Mental Health Consequences The COVID-19 pandemic has taken a psychological toll on special needs children and their caregivers. Negative emotions, changes in eating and sleeping patterns, and mood swings have put children at risk of developing a mental illness more quickly and exacerbating existing mental health problems (Holmes, et al., 2020). The lack of services provided in school and the change in learning formats have had an impact on children's emotional states. According to research, keeping a structured routine helps special needs children develop discipline and improve their safety. These children are at a higher risk of experiencing a mental relapse due to the abrupt change in their daily routine. The closure of schools and the shift to online learning platforms, according to Patel (2020), has increased stress and anxiety among special needs children and their parents. Mental health clinics and support systems have been closed or made inaccessible as the focus has shifted to the prevention and management of COVID-19. Parents and guardians face the challenge of assisting their special needs children in participating in online classes while also caring for them. Parents, it is widely believed, should be able to teach their children. This expectation raises their stress and anxiety levels, which in turn affects the kids. Dhiman et al. (2020) conducted a study to assess the impact of the COVID-19 pandemic on the mental health of special needs children and caregivers and found a high prevalence of depression. According to the researchers, the sudden closure of schools and imposition of a lockdown made it difficult for special needs children to access assistive services such as therapies, putting the burden on caregivers. It can be difficult for parents and caregivers to shift from their daily routine to providing specialised assistance, which can lead to caregiver stress. 13 Consequences for the Home Support System Most of the technologies and devices used to implement home-based distance learning are unfamiliar to some parents. Furthermore, the COVID-19 pandemic's tough economic conditions have made it difficult for most families to obtain the devices and internet necessary for online learning (Tokatly et al., 2020). Due to work overload, parents have insufficient time to monitor their disabled children, who miss out on the online learning process (Dhiman et al., 2020). Educators must recognise that making the abrupt transition to home-based learning is a challenge for many caregivers who are already stressed. As a result, as they work to reach out to students, they must also assist parents in learning how to use the technology that enables online learning. Only if parents are familiar with the entire infrastructure can they provide the necessary support to their children. As a result, in order to provide a meaningful learning experience, online learning programmes have had to form a working partnership with caregivers. Learners' ability to complete all lessons has been harmed by changes in learning processes and a lack of teaching skills from the home support system, resulting in incomplete tasks. The child's focus may deteriorate as a result of the incomplete tasks. Many children remained disconnected from their teachers as a result of the Covid-19 pandemic's abrupt changes, whereas others developed a positive relationship with their teachers. Disparities in access and retention of knowledge among children have resulted from the various levels of student-teacher connection. In addition, the disconnect between learners and the learning process has left some children befuddled, with the majority of them unable to communicate their feelings to caregivers and other family members (Tokatly et al., 2020). Caregivers may not understand the strategy used when assigning duties and responsibilities to special children, resulting in an overload of tasks. 14 Shifting to online learning has become a new way of learning, resulting in misunderstandings and confusion during lessons. Students' learning time has been reduced as a result of the COVID-19 pandemic, which has had a negative impact on their performance. Due to insufficient monitoring during the virtual learning era, new skills learned prior to the pandemic have been disrupted. Students' performance and skill development will suffer in the long run if they miss their learning sessions frequently. Maintaining and stimulating school-home partnerships is critical for children's achievement during the Covid-19 pandemic (Tremmel et al., 2020). Teachers' attitudes may have an impact on parents' involvement in their children's education; as a result, school leaders, teachers, and psychologists should take family-focused approaches to ensure that remote learning at home runs smoothly. The primary goal of the educational institution should be to meet with parents and guide them in supporting their children's online education. Furthermore, educational programmes implemented by schools can assist parents in coping with stress and connect families to community resources. Instilling a sense of responsibility in parents by communicating their roles and responsibilities during the pandemic (a higher level of parental involvement in their children's learning at home) may help to motivate learners (Petretto et al., 2020). Effects on Students' Capabilities Students' disengagement with learning has caused them to lose interest and focus, which could make school resumption difficult following the pandemic. The lack of requirements for effective remote learning has hampered the teaching of special needs children. Resuming in-person learning after the pandemic will be a challenge for students, teachers, and parents, as in-person learning is gradually being replaced by virtual learning. As a result, students must be psychologically prepared; it is possible that they will return to school soon (Joline E, et al., 2020). According to a study by 15 Stifel et al. (2020), online learning poses a challenge in how school psychologists conduct mental health assessments of students. The study proposes an assessment protocol that will allow psychologists to fulfil their responsibilities without endangering students' lives. The emotional, social, mental, and skill development of children is aided by personal relationships between students, teachers, and after-school activities. Prior to the pandemic, disabled children with physical and mental health issues could receive medical care at school-based clinics. Parents are concerned about the pandemic's long-term effects on special needs children, according to Neece et al. (2020), because most parents struggle to care for them at home. According to the study, special needs children who require specialised care will have their health deteriorated because these services are difficult to obtain during lockdowns. According to the findings, special needs children had unequal access to online learning and assessment. During the pandemic, testing and monitoring special children has become difficult, affecting students' performance and learning. However, the study found that not all is lost as a result of the pandemic, as 49.2 percent of the parents polled said they were able to spend more time with their children as a result of it. Due to the closure of schools as a result of the COVID-19 pandemic, special needs children have been deprived of basic needs that were previously available to them through schools (Tokatly Latzer et al., 2020). Schools can provide a comprehensive support system for special needs students, allowing them to thrive. While at school, children with autism can develop a healthy eating pattern, which is largely disrupted by school closures. Many parents in the study reported that their children's anxiety and stress as a result of the disruption resulted in refusal, food selectivity, and binge eating in some cases. It was difficult to obtain various foods in areas where families were not allowed to travel more than 330 feet from their homes. Unhealthy eating was caused by refusal, 16 selective eating, and a lack of food variety among special needs children. Additionally, when schools are open, some public schools provide students with free or reduced-price meals, which is not possible when schools are closed. Children from food-insecure families are deprived of these benefits, resulting in malnutrition or an unbalanced diet. Furthermore, some parents have lost their jobs and are unable to provide balanced diets to their children because they do not qualify for unemployment insurance (Fry-Bowers, 2020). Through online platforms, progressive monitoring of special education students can be carried out throughout the COVI19 closures. During distance learning, a partnership can provide students with modified goals (Peterson et al., 2020). School administrators can keep an eye on students with special needs to see if they are ready to return to school. Concerning COVID-19 closures related to special education, the office of special education programmes can provide information to caregivers and schools (Peterson et al., 2020). Volunteers can assist with home learning guidance and provide monitoring and support for students during the school day. During these unprecedented times, teachers can adjust the tracking of resources and guidance documents to provide the best education for students with disabilities. Maintaining regular physical activities and exercise in a safe home environment, especially for children with special needs, can be an important strategy for a healthy life during the Covid-19 crises. Children with disabilities benefit from physical activity because it improves their health and learning. Physical activities can help children with special needs improve their social behaviour, communication skills, and quality of life, reducing aggressive behaviour, stress, and behavioural problems during the pandemic (Yarmkaya & Esentürk, 2020). Lockdown restrictions put in place to stop the spread of the virus have been found to have reduced physical activity levels by more than 61 percent, according to research (Theis et al., 2021). Reduced physical activity 17 causes social and learning regression, as well as poor behaviour, in children with physical and intellectual disabilities. As a result, for disabled children who have no access to physical activities, teachers should work with caregivers to develop programmes that will keep them physically active while also keeping them safe. Massage and indoor workout activities are examples of such programmes. A daily visual schedule can help children with special needs establish a home routine as they become accustomed to new practises (Masonbrink & Hurley, 2020). Children can stay up to date by looking at the calendar every day and anticipating events. Days and weeks blend together without a typical school and weekend schedule, causing activities to become disoriented. Before moving on to the next exercise, children can use visual timers to see how much time is left for a specific action.

Hoping for a soft transition from online to face to face lessons

There is no set date for the pandemic to end or for face-to-face learning to resume. Teachers and caregivers must keep learners informed of any changes in the learning routine in the face of uncertainty. The return of in-person learning will have a negative impact on some learners' routines and learning because they have grown accustomed to home-based learning. As a result, educators and other stakeholders must adequately prepare students for an inclusive return to school. UNICEF proposes a seven-step 23 model in its 2020 report to ensure that schools achieve an inclusive return to school (UNICEF, 2020). Before reopening schools, learning institutions must develop clear plans to accept students back to school, allocate funds for special needs students, conduct outreach to families, and improve accessibility. In order to prepare for future closures, ensure that prevention protocols are in place, policies that promote quality education are implemented, and more money is invested in all-inclusive remote learning programmes. In terms of curriculum and assessment, the model proposes making learning materials available to students and communicating any curricular or assessment changes that will be implemented once schools reopen. Before schools are reopened to the support system, the model proposes additional training for special needs teachers as well as mental health support. Following the reopening of the schools, clear protection protocols for teachers and students should be implemented. In addition, schools should create a welcoming learning environment to help students make the transition from at-home to in-school learning. Finally, collaboration and monitoring will ensure that all children with disabilities are able to return to school. The safety of students should be a top priority in any return to school plan for children with disabilities. Return to school programmes, according to Joline et al. (2020), should focus on providing a safe and less restrictive learning environment for staff and students. According to this study, learning institutions must adequately prepare for the reopening of schools in order to avoid challenges in the transition to online learning. Because children with disabilities may have difficulty understanding and adhering to established healthcare protocols, schools must take steps to ensure that these students are closely monitored and assisted in order to ensure their safety. In addition, while enforcing healthcare protocols to stop the virus from spreading, schools must avoid isolating students. Social isolation in any form has a significant impact on learners with disabilities. Isolating students with emotional and cognitive disabilities from activities like singing and playing will deprive them of their only opportunity for meaningful social interaction with others. As a result, it is critical to consider the needs of individual students as schools strive to follow safety protocols. The problem of determining the most appropriate opening strategy for students with disabilities is a challenge that schools face in collaboration with other stakeholders. Students with disabilities, according to Joline et al. (2020), benefit more from in-person learning because their learning necessitates specialised interaction with special needs teachers and other professionals. They are, however, at a higher risk of contracting COVID-19 because they are unable to comprehend and follow prevention protocols without supervision. As a result, Agoratus (2020) recommends a phased return to in-person learning that takes into account the risk levels of both teachers and students. Furthermore, schools should include community participation in determining the best back-to-school programme, according to Carvalho et al. (2020). The approach to back-to-school should be child-centred. Following the reopening of schools, education disruption is likely to continue, with the possibility of future closures. As a result, students should be involved in every stage of the school's reopening. Children with disabilities may resist returning to school because they are resistant to change in their lives. Although resistance is acceptable, educators and parents can overcome it by providing reopening plans prior to returning to school. Learners with disabilities should be considered in new in-person regulations. For example, Moro et al. (2020) suggest that when setting up hand hygiene stations, schools should consider including support for special needs students. Educators should also continue to explain to students why they can't learn the way they used to, why they must wear masks, wash their hands frequently, and maintain social distance. In addition, 25 students must be taught what will happen if they do not follow the new regulations. Creating a routine around these changes will aid learners in quickly adapting to the new changes. As a result, involving learners at every stage of the transition will ensure that the transition is quick and painless.

Virtual Education for Special Children during the Pandemic

Ashwini M.Madawana

Ministry Of Health Malaysia

nairm794@gmail.com

Ananthi Gurusamy

Ministry of Education Malaysia

ananthigurusamy@gmail.com

ABSTRACT

The shift from face-to-face to online learning increases stress and workload for special needs educators. Suicide rates have reportedly doubled from January to April of 2021 due to population adaptation issues during the Pandemic. This study seeks to discover what was done to help disabled people continue their education while the pandemic ravaged the country. It will assess how educational advancements helped disabled children and their families. The sampling method would have parameters. Due to the Pandemic and Movement Control Restrictions, rapid case sampling is thought to be beneficial. The study collects data through semi-structured interviews. We'll interview the special education director at each school. In their interviews, teachers discuss the distance learning programme, how it incorporates special education software, and their own suggestions.

Keywords: COVID-19, Children with Special Needs, Special Needs Educators, Learning

1.INTRODUCTION

Special Needs Children are certified by a doctor, optician, audiologist, or psychologist. Special education is the teaching of students with special needs. Open and Distance Learning (ODL) is a method where teachers and students can work together remotely. It is flexible in terms of teaching and learning methods. In general, teachers, students, and parents struggle with the abrupt shift to online learning. Adaptive technology is new to special ed Teaching with technology is impossible for teachers. Teachers should learn their students' software and routines. Many reasons exist for teaching special needs students differently (Altinay, Altinay, Dagli, and Altinay, 2018). Distance learning may be considered for students whose developmental levels vary by age group. However, students with special needs who develop at different rates should also get special training (Çelikten, 2018). Providing accessible technologies and information can help students with disabilities learn. These students require more specialised education. Education for students with developmental differences. This research will examine what distance education accomplishes and how students can benefit from it (Zhang, et al., 2020).

2. NEED FOR STUDY

The Ministry of National Education launched distance education applications with the help of volunteer teachers. Absent an open education policy, all levels of education emphasise distance learning. No local action plan means that all institutions, including teachers, are looking for ways to better recover. This programme fosters collegiality by providing an alternative platform for learners and teachers to interact (Huang, et al, 2020). This study supports Gilly Salmon's Carpe Diem model's regional action plans and special needs action plans. Encouraging family education isn't enough. Leadership and technology selection are critical during pandemics. Teachers must learn students' software and routines to help them adjust. Stress and anxiety can lead to depression. They must also create a syllabus or teaching methods that are specific to each student. Students must benefit from teachers' efforts. Evaluating months of integration for flaws, errors, or improvements is required. Unreviewed educational systems fail with unintended consequences

3. BACKGROUND

A lot of research is done on caregivers' mental health and telerehabilitation usage. 62.5 percent had symptoms of depression, anxiety, or stress. caregiver strain was significantly different from baseline (p0.001, effect size=0.93) (pre-outbreak strain was measured retrospectively). A lack of or dissatisfaction with tele-rehabilitation was linked to psychological symptoms and strain among caregivers who did not use it. 75% of people felt stressed or depressed (Dhiman, 2020). In a study, Filipino teachers faced educational, socialisation, and psychological issues COVID-19's disruption of classrooms causes issues for SEND students. Teachers also struggle to adapt to and meet SEND students' needs. A pandemic view of inclusive education teachers' challenges, strategies and future.The researcher emailed and chatted with five Filipino special education teachers [(Toquero, 2021)]. For this study, a mixed-methods approach was used to gather information from parochial and private school teachers. Teachers range in age from 25 to over 50 and are technologically savvy. Teachers were expected to teach daily synchronous online classes and complete synchronous and asynchronous assignments. Teachers either received inadequate or no training on online video conferencing platforms and teaching tools. They taught for less time and offered daily virtual office hours to help students. Tuition-paying parents had high expectations for curriculum, teaching quality, and student engagement. Parents observed teachers in action. Depending on the child's age, parents were frequently required to force their child to attend class. Teachers were dissatisfied with their schools' technology and unprepared for change. Due to time constraints and new delivery methods, they struggled to meet parental expectations. Many employees and students felt isolated. Parents and administrators expect teachers to meet students' individual needs. Individual support meant longer teaching hours and ignoring individual needs. (A.2020). In contrast to Chao et al. (2006), McLean (2006) emphasises the critical nature of direct feedback in online learning environments. This study found that some distance education applications developed for elementary school students could be used to educate children with disabilities during an epidemic period, and that distance education applications are critical to ensure that children with disabilities do not withdraw from school as quickly as their peers (Özdilekler, Altınay, Altınay, & Dagli,2018)

4. RESEARCH OBJECTIVES As the epidemic spreads, this research seeks to answer what is done in distance education and how students can benefit from it. RO1 Evaluate the Open and Distance Learning programme. RO2 Evaluate the Special Needs Teaching Applications. RO3 Determine if changes are required to improve learning for Special Needs Children.

5. RESEARCH QUESTIONS

RQ1 Is Open and Distance Learning Beneficial for Special Needs Children?

RQ2 Is the Special Needs Teaching application useful?

RQ3 Are there any changes that should be made to the Open and Distance Learning for Special Needs programme to benefit children with disabilities?

6. METHODOLOGY

This is a qualitative research project. Simple case sampling method would be used. A popular qualitative research method is on-the-spot interviews (Yldrm & Imşek, 2013). Specific sampling parameters are required by the Pandemic and Movement Control Restrictions. Semi-structured interviews will be used in the study. The special education teachers at each school will be interviewed. Questions about distance learning, special education software, and teacher ideas reveal the general consensus. Researchers can easily contact teachers during an outbreak.

7. RESEARCH TIMELINE

The project is expected to take 17 weeks to complete, with the following activity durations listed for each section of the research project:

Research Section	Duration
1. Title	1 week
2. Introduction	1 week

3. Need for this Study	2 weeks
4. Background	3 weeks
5. Objectives	1 week
6. Research Questions and or Hypothesis	1 week
7. Research Methodology	2 weeks
8. Data analysis interpretations and discussions	3 weeks
9. Summary conclusion and recommendations	2 weeks
10.Reviewing work for final submission	1 week

CITATION AND REFERENCES

A. (2020). Global pandemic contorts traditional classroom teaching for private school | 14th International Multi- Conference on Society, Cybernetics and Informatics, IMSCI 2020;: 187–190, 2020. | Scopus. World health organization -covid-19 global literature on coronavirus disease. https://pesquisa.bvsalud.org/global-literature-on-novel-coronavirus-2019-ncov/resource/en/covidwho- 950549

Agoratus, L. (2020). Extended school year and compensatory services: Special education during the COVID-19 pandemic. The Exceptional Parent, 50(6), 22.

Altinay, F., Altinay, M., Dagli, G., and Altinay, Z. (2018). "Being leader in global citizenship at the information technology age" Qual Quant, 52(1). Doi: 10.1007/s11135-017-0585

Altinay, F., Altinay, Z. Dagli, G. Cifci, M. (2018). "Evaluation of administrative and supervisory performance of the directors of special education institutions according to the teachers" Quality & Quantity. 52(2), 1275- 1286.

Buchnat, M., & Wojciechowska, A. (2020). Online education of students with mild intellectual disability and autism spectrum disorder during the COVID-19 pandemic. Interdyscyplinarne Konteksty Pedagogiki Specjalnej, (29), 149-171. Doi:10.14746/ikps.2020.29.07

Çelikten. M., & Özkan, H. H. (2018). Teacher performance evaluation system. Opus- International Journal of Society Researches, 8(15), 806-824. Doi: 10. 26466/opus. 418565.

Chao, T, Saj, T. Ve Tessier, F. (2006). Establishing a quality review for online courses. Educause quarterly, 3, 32- https://net.educause.edu/ir/library/pdf/eqm0635.pdf

Chetty, R., Hendren, N., Kline, P., & Saez, E. (2013). The equality of opportunity project. Summary of project findings, July. Retrieved from http://obs.rc.fas.harvard.edu/chetty/ website/IGE/Executive%20Summary.pdf

Clinton, H. R. (1996). It takes a village. New York, NY: Simon & Schuster.

CONROY, P. (2012). COLLABORATING WITH CULTURAL AND LINGUISTICALLY DIVERSE FAMILIES OF STUDENTS IN RURAL SCHOOLS WHO RECEIVE SPECIAL EDUCATION SERVICES. RURAL SPECIAL EDUCATION QUARTERLY, 31(3), 20-24

DHIMAN, S. (2020). IMPACT OF COVID-19 OUTBREAK ON MENTAL HEALTH AND PERCEIVED STRAIN AMONG CAREGIVERS TENDING CHILDREN WITH SPECIAL NEEDS. PUBMED. HTTPS://PUBMED.NCBI.NLM.NIH.GOV/33091712/

DOOLEY, D. G., SIMPSON, J. N., & BEERS, N. S. (2020). RETURNING TO SCHOOL IN THE ERA OF COVID19. JAMA PEDIATRICS, 174(11), 1028-1029. DOI:10.1001/JAMAPEDIATRICS.2020.3874

DUNST, C. J., TRIVETTE, C. M., & HAMBY, D. W. (2006). FAMILY SUPPORT PROGRAM QUALITY AND PARENT, FAMILY AND CHILD BENEFITS. ASHEVILLE, NC: WINTERBERRY PRESS.

DUNST, C. J., TRIVETTE, C. M., & HAMBY, D. W. (2007). META-ANALYSIS OF FAMILY-CENTERED HELP GIVING PRACTICES RESEARCH.

ESPE-SHERWINDT, M. (2008). FAMILY-CENTRED PRACTICE: COLLABORATION, COMPETENCY AND EVIDENCE. SUPPORT FOR LEARNING, 23(3), 136-143.

FLEMONS, D. (1991). COMPLETING DISTINCTIONS. BOSTON, MA: SHAMBHALA.

FLEMONS, D. (2002). OF ONE MIND: THE LOGIC OF HYPNOSIS, THE PRACTICE OF THERAPY. NEW YORK, NY: W. W. NORTON.

FREDERICK, J. K., RAABE, G. R., ROGERS, V. R., & PIZZICA, J. (2020). ADVOCACY, COLLABORATION, AND INTERVENTION: A MODEL OF DISTANCE SPECIAL EDUCATION SUPPORT SERVICES AMID COVID-19. BEHAVIOR ANALYSIS IN PRACTICE, 1-9. DOI:HTTPS://DOI.ORG/10.1007/S40617-020-00476-1

FRY-BOWERS, E. K. (2020). CHILDREN ARE AT RISK FROM COVID-19. JOURNAL OF PEDIATRIC NURSING, 53, A10-A12. DOI:10.1016/J.PEDN.2020.04.026

GOLDSCHMIDT, K. (2020). THE COVID-19 PANDEMIC: TECHNOLOGY USE TO SUPPORT THE WELLBEING OF CHILDREN. JOURNAL OF PEDIATRIC NURSING, 88–90. DOI:10.1016/J.PEDN.2020.04.013

GUIDANCE ON ACTIVE LEARNING AT HOME DURING EDUCATIONAL DISRUPTION: PROMOTING STUDENT'S SELF-REGULATION SKILLS DURING COVID-19 OUTBREAK. BEIJING: SMART LEARNING INSTITUTE OF BEIJING NORMAL UNIVERSITY

HARRY, B. (2008). COLLABORATION WITH CULTURALLY AND LINGUISTICALLY DIVERSE FAMILIES: IDEAL VS. REALITY. EXCEPTIONAL CHILDREN, 74(3), 372388.

HEALY, A. L., KEESEE, P. D., & SMITH, B. S. (1989). EARLY SERVICES FOR CHILDREN WITH SPECIAL NEEDS: TRANSACTIONS FOR FAMILY SUPPORT. BALTIMORE, MD: BROOKES.

HOLMES, E. A., PERRY, V. H., TRACEY, I., WESSELY, S., ARSENEAULT, L., & BULLMORE, E. (2020). MULTIDISCIPLINARY RESEARCH PRIORITIES FOR THE COVID-19 PANDEMIC: A CALL FOR ACTION FOR 28 MENTAL HEALTH SCIENCE. THE LANCET PSYCHIATRY, 7(6), 547-560. DOI:HTTPS://DOI.ORG/10.1016/S2215-0366(20)30168-1

HUANG, R.H., LIU, D.J., ZHAN, T., AMELINA, N., YANG, J.F., ZHUANG, R.X., CHANG, T.W., & CHENG, W. (2020).

IDEA. (2004). Title I, part A, section 601. Retrieved from http://idea.ed.gov/explore/view/p/% 2Croot%2Cstatute%2CI%2CA%2C601%2C

Iivari, N., Sharma, S., & Ventä-Olkkonen, L. (2020). Digital transformation of everyday life– how COVID-19 pandemic transformed the basic education of the young generation and why information management research should care? International Journal of Information Management, 55, 102183. Doi:https://doi.org/10.1016/j.ijinfomgt.2020.102183

Iyer, P. (2013). Where is home? TedTalk. Retrieved from http://www.ted.com/talks/pico_iyer_ where_is_home

Jameson, J. M., Stegenga, S. M., Ryan, J., & Green, A. (2020). Free appropriate public education in the time of COVID-19. Rural Special Education Quarterly, 39(4), 181- 192. Doi:https://doi.org/10.1177/8756870520959659

Joline E, B., Lainie K, H., Susan D, A., Amy J, H., Robert, R., & Maurice G, S. (2020). School reopening during COVID-19 pandemic: Considering students with disabilities. Journal of Pediatric Rehabilitation Medicine, 1-7. Doi:10.3233/PRM-200789

Klapproth, F., Federkeil, L., Heinschke, F., & Jungmann, T. (2020). Teachers' experiences of stress and their coping strategies during COVID-19 induced distance teaching. Journal of Pedagogical Research, 4(4), 444-452. Doi:https://doi.org/10.33902/JPR.2020062805

Kong, M., & Thompson, L. A. (2020). Considerations for young children and those with special needs as COVID-19 continues. JAMA pediatrics, 174(10), 1012-1012. Doi:10.1001/jamapediatrics.2020.2478

Masonbrink, A. R., & Hurley, E. (2020). Advocating for children during the COVID-19 school closures. Pediatrics, 146(3), e20201440. Doi:https://doi.org/10.1542/peds.2020-1440

McLean, J. (2006). "Forgotten Faculty: Stress and Job Satisfaction among Distance Educators" Online Journal of Distance Learning Administration, Vol. 9 No. 2.

M Madawana, Ashwini and Gurusamy, Ananthi, Virtual Education for Special Children during the Pandemic (September 10, 2021). Available at SSRN: https://ssrn.com/abstract=3921920 or http://dx.doi.org/10.2139/ssrn.3921920

Mueller, J. T., McConnell, K., Burow, P. B., Pofahl, K., Merdjanoff, A. A., & Farrell, J. (2021). Impacts of the COVID-19 pandemic on rural America. Proceedings of the National Academy of Sciences, 118(1), 2019378118. Retrieved from https://doi.org/10.1073/pnas.2019378118

Mutluer, T., Doenyas, C., & Genc, H. A. (2020). Behavioral implications of the COVID-19 process for autism spectrum disorder, and individuals' comprehension of and reactions to the pandemic conditions. Frontiers in psychiatry, 11, 561882. Retrieved from https://doi.org/10.3389/fpsyt.2020.561882

Nazerian, T. (2020). Impact of the COVID-19 pandemic on early childhood care and education. Early Child Educ J., 1-4. Doi:10.1007/s10643-020-01082-0

Neece, c., mcintyre, l. L., & fenning, r. (2020). Examining the impact of covid-19 in ethnically diverse families with young children with intellectual and developmental disabilities. Journal of intellectual disability research, 64(10), 739-749. Doi:https://doi.org/10.1111/jir.12769

Özdilekler, m.a.; altinay, f.; altinay, z.; dagli g. (2018). "an evaluation of class-teachers' roles in transferring values" quality & quantity, 52(2)

Paterson, k. (2010). Teaching in troubled times. Markham, ontario: pembroke publishers. Pdk/gallup. (2014). The pdk/gallup poll of the public's attitudes toward the public schools, september. Retrieved from http://pdkpoll.pdkintl.org/#9 pisa. (2012). Retrieved from http://www.oecd.org/pisa/keyfindings/pisa-2012-results-overview.pdf

Patel, k. (2020). Mental health implications of covid-19 on children with disabilities. Asian journal of psychiatry, 102273. Doi:10.1016/j.ajp.2020.102273 petretto, d. r., masala, i., & masala, c. (2020). Special educational needs, distance learning, inclusion and covid-19. Prior, s. p. (2020, may). Covid-19 cannot quarantine special education rights. Retrieved from ep-magazine.

Rattigan-rohr, j. (2012). It takes a village: a collaborative assault on the struggling reader dilemma. Rotterdam: sense publishers. Satir, v. (1972). Peoplemaking. Palo alto, ca: science and behavior.

Reich, j., buttimer, c. J., fang, a., hillaire, g., hirsch, k., larke, l. R., & slama, r. (n.d.). Remote learning guidance from state education agencies during the covid-19 pandemic: a first look. Doi:https://doi.org/10.35542/osf.io/437e2

Schon, d. A. (1983). The reflective practitioner: how professionals think in action. New york, ny: basic books.

Schaeffer, k. (2020, april 23). As schools shift to online learning amid pandemic, here's what we know about disabled students in the u.s. retrieved from pew research center. 30

Spann, s. J., kohler, f. W., & soenksen, d. (2003). Examining parents' involvement in and perceptions of special education services: an interview with families in a parent support group. Focus autism other developmental disabilities, 4(18), 228237. Doi:10.1177/ 10883576030180040401

Stenhoff, d. M., pennington, r. C., & tapp, m. C. (2020). Distance education support for students with autism spectrum disorder and complex needs during covid-19 and school closures. Rural special education quarterly, 39(4), 211-219. Doi:https://doi.org/10.1177/8756870520959658

Stifel, s. W., feinberg, d. K., zhang, y., chan, m. K., & wagle, r. (2020). Assessment during the covid-19 pandemic: ethical, legal, and safety considerations moving forward. School psychology review, 49(4), 438-452. Doi:https://doi.org/10.1080/2372966x.2020.1844549

Taylor, h., krane, d., & orkis, k. (2010). The ada, 20 years later: executive summary, july. Retrieved from

HTTP://NOD.ORG/ASSETS/DOWNLOADS/2010_SURVEY_OF_AMERICANS_WITH_DISABILITIES_GAPS_FULL_REPORT.PDF

THE ROLE OF COMMUNITY IN SPECIAL EDUCATION: A RELATIONAL APPROACH | EMERALD INSIGHT. (2015). EMERALD. HTTPS://WWW.EMERALD.COM/INSIGHT/CONTENT/DOI/10.1108/S0270-401320150000030A008/FULL/HTML

TOKATLY LATZER, I., LEITNER, Y., & KARNIELI-MILLER, O. (2021). CORE EXPERIENCES OF PARENTS OF CHILDREN WITH AUTISM DURING THE COVID-19 PANDEMIC LOCKDOWN. AUTISM, 136236132098431 7. RETRIEVED FROM HTTPS://DOI.ORG/10.1177/1362361320984317

TOQUERO, C. M. D. (2021, MARCH 30). 'SANA ALL' INCLUSIVE EDUCATION AMID COVID-19: CHALLENGES, STRATEGIES, AND PROSPECTS OF SPECIAL EDUCATION TEACHERS |INTERNATIONAL AND MULTIDISCIPLINARY JOURNAL OF SOCIAL SCIENCES.INTERNATIONAL AND MULTIDISCIPLINARY JOURNAL IN SOCIAL SCIENCES. HTTPS://HIPATIAPRESS.COM/HPJOURNALS/INDEX.PHP/RIMCIS/ARTICLE/VIEW/631

TREMMEL, P., MYERS, R., BRUNOW, D. A., & HOTT, B. L. (2020). EDUCATING STUDENTS WITH DISABILITIES DURING THE COVID-19 PANDEMIC: LESSONS LEARNED FROM COMMERCE INDEPENDENT SCHOOL DISTRICT. RURAL SPECIAL EDUCATION QUARTERLY, 39(4), 201-210. RETRIEVED FROM HTTPS://DOI.ORG/10.1177/8756870520958114

TURNBULL, A., TURNBULL, R., ERWIN, E., & SODAK, L. (2006). FAMILIES, PROFESSIONALS, AND EXCEPTIONALITY: COLLABORATING FOR EMPOWERMENT. UPPER SADDLE RIVER, NJ: PRENTICE-HALL.

UNICEF. (N.D.). CHILDREN WITH DISABILITIES. RETRIEVED FROM UNICEF: HTTPS://WWW.UNICEF.ORG/ECA/CHILDREN-DISABILITIES

VILLA, K., & THOUSAND, J. (1988). ENHANCING SUCCESS IN HETEROGENEOUS CLASSROOM AND SCHOOLS: THE POWER OF PARTNERSHIPS. TEACHER EDUCATION AND SPECIAL EDUCATION, 11, 144-154.

WATZLAWICK, P., WEAKLAND, J., & FISCH, R. (1974). CHANGE: PRINCIPLES OF PROBLEM FORMATION AND PROBLEM RESOLUTION. NEW YORK, NY: W. W. NORTON.

WEISS, H. B., & STEPHEN, N. (2009). FROM PERIPHERY TO CENTER: A NEW VISION FOR FAMILY, SCHOOL, AND COMMUNITY PARTNERSHIPS. IN S. CHRISTENSON & A. RESCHLEY (EDS.), HANDBOOK OF SCHOOLFAMILY PARTNERSHIPS (PP. 448472). NEW YORK, NY: ROUTLEDGE.

WELCH, M., & SHERIDAN, S. M. (1995). EDUCATIONAL PARTNERSHIPS: SERVING STUDENTS AT RISK. FORT WORTH, TX: HARCOURT BRACE

WONG, C. A., MING, D., MASLOW, G., & GIFFORD, E. J. (2020). MITIGATING THE IMPACTS OF THE COVID-19 PANDEMIC RESPONSE ON AT-RISK CHILDREN. PEDIATRICS, 146(1), E20200973.

YARIMKAYA, E., & ESENTÜRK, O. K. (2020). PROMOTING PHYSICAL ACTIVITY FOR CHILDREN WITH AUTISM SPECTRUM DISORDERS DURING CORONAVIRUS OUTBREAK: BENEFITS, STRATEGIES, AND EXAMPLES. INTERNATIONAL JOURNAL OF DEVELOPMENTAL DISABILITIES, 1-6. DOI:HTTPS://DOI.ORG/10.1080/20473869.2020.1756115

Yildirim, A. & Simsek, H. (2013). Qualitative research methods. Ankara: Seçkin Publishing

Zhang, X., Tlili, A., Nascimbeni, F. et al. (2020). Accessibility within open educational resources and practices for disabled learners: a systematic literature review. Smart Learning Environments, 7, 1. https://doi.org/10.1186/s40561-019-0113

www.ingramcontent.com/pod-product-compliance
Lightning Source LLC
LaVergne TN
LVHW052106160826
845678LV00015B/3390

* 9 7 9 8 4 8 1 3 3 4 1 9 6 *